AI and the Gig Economy

Opportunities and Challenges for Freelancers

Table of Contents

Chapter 1. Introduction

In our latest Special Report, we peel back the layers of an emerging trend that is fundamentally reconstructing the nature of work: AI and the Gig Economy. As technology wields its influence over traditional modes of employment, a new landscape opens to freelancers filled with unprecedented opportunities, yet not without its own unique set of challenges. This is not about fantastical visions of the future, but rather, a grounded assessment of today's digital-led gig economy. As we dive into the nuances of AI in fostering freelance work, we also bring focus on aiding independent workers navigate successfully in this brave new world. This exceptional report is informative and engaging - a must-have for every freelancer aiming for success in the digital world!

Chapter 2. The Emergence of AI in the Gig Economy

The dawn of the Internet Age introduced to the world the concept of the gig economy - transient work characterized by flexible, temporary or freelance jobs. With the ascendancy of advanced artificial intelligence (AI) technologies, this landscape is primed for even more dramatic change. Let's take a journey into this evolving world and consider both its stunning prospects and potential challenges.

2.1. AI: Reshaping Work and Opportunities

Artificial intelligence has marked its presence in a variety of industries, from healthcare, real estate, and retail to transport. Its value lies in its innate capacity to learn and improve upon tasks, making it a valuable asset in the world of labor where adaptability and efficiency are king.

In the gig economy, AI has a transformative role, primarily in three ways. First, by fueling platforms that connect freelancers to potential projects fitting their skills and preferences. Second, optimizing the workflow for the gig worker through smart tools like project management apps, automated scheduling, and even AI-driven content creation. Third, AI advances have allowed the evolution of work traditionally done by humans to now be performed by AI, birthing new gig opportunities such as collecting and analyzing datasets used to train AI models, a sort of 'blue-collar' AI work.

2.2. AI-Fueled Platforms: Bridging Gaps in the Gig Economy

In a manifestation of the "network effect," as gig economy platforms have grown, so has the number of opportunities for freelancers. Using data-driven algorithms, these platforms can match freelancers with relevant job postings, increase their visibility to potential clients, and even help set competitive prices for their services. The use of AI in crafting a rewarding experience for freelancers on these platforms is an ongoing development.

Perhaps the best form of AI application comes from advanced matching algorithms. Artificial intelligence can analyze multiple aspects of a freelancer's profile - skills, experience, rates, availability, and more - to connect them with the best-suited jobs. By absorbing vast amounts of information and patterns in the data, AI can enhance matching efficiency while eliminating much of the guesswork for the freelancer.

Notably, AI has ushered in benefits for those seeking freelance work. It enables higher income potential, flexible work hours, work-life balance, enriched job satisfaction, and increased productivity. Although AI has been instrumental in unlocking unparalleled opportunities, it isn't a silver bullet that solves all the gig economy challenges.

2.3. Navigating Challenges in AI-Driven Gig Economy

While AI is essentially a force for good in the gig economy, it's not without its hurdles. One significant challenge arises from algorithmic decision-making, which, while efficient, can sometimes lack the human touch needed in certain circumstances. A hiring algorithm can't fully appreciate—or perhaps even recognize—the freelancer's soft skills, like leadership, empathy, or effective communication, that can make the difference in many professional settings.

Moreover, gig workers are often tasked with training the AI that might eventually render their services obsolete. At face value, this seems like a perverse arrangement; however, it underscores the complex relationship between freelance workers and AI technologies. It's essential to counterbalance the reality that with AI's growth comes displacement. Therefore, it's crucial for gig workers to continuously learn, adapt, and remain agile in this rapidly transforming landscape.

2.4. Looking Forward

As AI continues to reshape the gig economy, it's worth pondering what the future holds. For instance, as AI technologies become increasingly sophisticated, opportunities for gig work could diminish, and the balance of power could shift even further towards those who own and control these powerful tools.

However, instead of viewing AI as a threat, freelancers can see it as a tool to heighten their competitive edge. Future-forward education should focus on critical and creative thinking, problem-solving, and emotional intelligence – skills that even the most advanced AI lacks.

In conclusion, while the rise of artificial intelligence in the gig economy has ushered in a plethora of opportunities for businesses and freelancers alike, it also comes with unique challenges. The onus is now on policymakers, educators, gig workers, and the AI community to ensure that this transformation serves the majority and doesn't result in an undue concentration of wealth and power.

Chapter 3. Understanding the Gig Economy: Key Features and Characteristics

The gig economy refers to a labor market characterized by the prevalence of short-term contracts or freelance work, as opposed to permanent jobs. It's an evolving component of the labor market made up of solo entrepreneurs, project teams, temporary helpers, contractors, and freelancers. Besides, with the rising trend of digital platforms, the gig workforce is also growing.

3.1. Understanding the Prevalence of Gig Economy

The gig economy has seen exponential growth over the past decade. The McKinsey Global Institute estimated in 2016 that 20 to 30 percent of the working-age population in the United States and the fifteen largest European economies engaged in independent work. These figures are continually increasing as more individuals are transitioning voluntarily to gig work due to the flexibility, autonomy, and diversified income streams it offers. A significant advantage of the gig economy is the ability to have multiple income streams, thereby enhancing financial security.

3.2. The Benefits of Engaging in the Gig Economy

A profound benefit of gig working is increased autonomy, allowing individuals to control their workload, working hours, and the type of work they accept. This autonomy often leads to greater job satisfaction as individuals can work in alignment with their strengths, skills, and passions.

Work flexibility is another key feature. The ability to set one's schedule, work from various locations, and balance work and life commitments makes the gig economy popular amongst various demographic groups. It includes single parents, caregivers, students, retirees, and those wishing to supplement income from traditional employment.

Moreover, the gig economy can provide opportunities for people to gain diverse work experiences, learn new skills, and build a broad portfolio. This versatility can enrich an individual's career and make them more attractive to future clients or employers.

3.3. Challenges Faced by Gig Workers

Yet, participating in the gig economy is not without its challenges. For one, there is the lack of traditional employment benefits such as health insurance, retirement contributions, and paid leave. This lack of security can add a layer of stress, especially in uncertain times. In some regions, independent contractors have little legal protection against unfair dismissal or non-payment for their work.

Additionally, gig work often requires a significant amount of self-marketing. Freelancers need to continually pursue new contracts, negotiate rates, and manage relationships with multiple clients simultaneously. Therefore, the gig economy demands strong self-management, marketing, negotiating, and networking skills that not all potential gig workers may possess or desire to develop.

Fluctuating-income is another characteristic of the gig economy, with work and earnings often being less predictable than in traditional employment. The ability to manage financial uncertainty is a critical skill for gig workers and can influence the overall experience and satisfaction of the gig economy.

3.4. Technological Innovations Driving the Gig Economy

In recent years, digital platforms such as Uber, Airbnb, TaskRabbit, and Upwork have driven significant expansion in the gig economy. These platforms match supply and demand for temporary work and have provided millions of individuals with new ways to work and earn income.

These platforms democratize work, allowing people to generate income using their resources or skills. With a vehicle, a person can become an Uber or Lyft driver. With a spare room, a person can become an Airbnb host. With accessible digital tools, one can offer freelance services in sectors such as design, programming, or content writing.

While these applications largely focus on low-skilled work or asset sharing, new platforms are increasingly catering to professional services. Websites such as Toptal, Catalant, and 10x Management offer platforms for highly skilled professionals to connect with businesses seeking their expertise.

3.5. The Future of Gig Economy

The intersection of the gig workforce and recent AI innovations marks a significant shift in work and labor markets. With advancements in artificial intelligence, some gig jobs may become automated, and others may change dramatically in scope and nature. However, the human element—creative thinking, complex problem solving, emotional intelligence—cannot be replaced, indicating that gig work is likely to proliferate rather than diminish.

In conclusion, the gig economy breaks free from traditional

employment models, igniting a new form of work that is shaping the economic landscape. It provides numerous benefits, including work flexibility and the opportunity to follow passions and interests but also presents unique challenges like income fluctuation and lack of benefits. It is crucial for those participating in the gig economy to understand these dynamics to successfully navigate and thrive in this evolving labor market.

Consequently, understanding these dynamics is crucial for anyone wishing to participate successfully in the gig economy. In the upcoming chapters, we'll delve deeper into the intersection of AI and the gig economy, illuminating the risks and benefits, tools and strategies, and future trends that might shape your career as a freelancer in the digital world.

Chapter 4. The Intersection of AI and Freelancing: A New Order

As this technological epoch unfolds, the intersection of Artificial Intelligence (AI) and freelancing presents a revolutionary transformation. The dawn of AI has ushered in a new realm of opportunities by morphing the traditional freelance landscape.

4.1. The Artificial Intelligence Impact

AI, with its breadth of inherent potentials, fosters a ground-breaking environment for the freelance workforce. Implementation of AI tools broadens new efficient horizons with mechanisms like automated assistance, improved customer service, advanced security systems, and streamlined workflows. The subsequent sections delve deeper into comprehending this impactful convergence.

4.2. Intelligent Assistance to Freelancers

AI-powered systems offer an array of benefits that immensely augment productivity for freelancers. Digital assistants, calendar software, and job matching algorithms are just a few among the myriad AI applications that lend a helping hand in managing mundane tasks, allowing freelancers more time to focus on the core of their work. Not only does this result in enhanced output quality, but the time saved particularly aids freelancers in juggling multiple projects seamlessly.

4.3. Job-Matching and Lead Generation

The intelligent algorithms of AI have the capability to scrutinize countless job postings and extract those that specifically align with a freelancer's skill set. Similarly, lead generation for freelance marketers has been elevated to a new level, with AI tackling intricate analysis to identify potential prospects.

4.4. Customer Service Enhancement

AI also provides customer service solutions that are quintessential for freelancers who aim to grow their clientele. Chatbots and automated responses, for instance, provide quick and effective customer support, accessible round the clock. This crucial aspect of customer service greatly enhances communication, subsequently fostering excellent client satisfaction and retention.

4.5. Heightened Security

For freelancers working in the digital space, AI-backed security systems provide an invaluable guard against potential data breaches and cyber threats. The inbuilt intelligence of these systems enables proactive threat detection and prevention, thus safeguarding the sensitive data that freelancers often deal with.

Despite these promising prospects, the intertwining of AI and freelancing does not come without its own set of challenges.

4.6. The Creeping Threat of Job Displacement

While AI brings about multiple productivity-enhancing possibilities, it also posits an alarming concern of job displacement. Automation could potentially lead to certain freelance tasks becoming obsolete, consequently threatening job security.

4.7. Data Security and Privacy

Even though AI offers superior security systems, issues around data protection and privacy are still prevalent. As freelancers frequently deal with classified data, the advent of AI-aggravated privacy threats cannot be dismissed lightly.

4.8. Closing the Skill Gap

The proliferation of AI in the freelancing space necessitates an adept understanding of the new tools and systems. Consequently, freelancers are left with the task of incessantly updating their skill set to stay competitive.

Looking forward, the integration of AI and freelancing signals an exciting path, teeming with both challenges and opportunities.

4.9. Aiding Successful Navigation

In this rapidly evolving ecosystem, various factors like freelancers' adaptability, evolving skill sets, continuous learning, and efficient use of available resources are instrumental in cultivating a successful career trajectory.

4.10. Unprecedented Opportunities

While AI might pose a threat to some traditional freelance jobs, it simultaneously creates a host of new opportunities. With performance-enhancing tools and streamlined processes, freelancers equipped with the right skills stand to capitalize on an evolving market space.

The integration of AI and freelancing has the potential to create a paradigm shift in the world of work. Despite the challenges laid bare, AI's strategic employment can undeniably usher freelancing to the next level. An adaptive mindset, coupled with continuous skill enhancement, and equipped understanding of AI tools will be prerequisites to seize the unlimited possibilities this new era promises.

The landscape is unveiling itself, the intersection of AI and freelancing is not just an emerging trend, but arguably the way forward. Only time will affirm this stance as we continue to delve into the depths of this fascinating amalgamation. This is just the initiation of what is yet to come, it, however, promises an intriguing journey with bountiful rewards.

Chapter 5. The Role of AI in Facilitating Freelance Work

Today's global economy has shifted gears in many sectors, responding to a mix of technological innovation, a changing workforce, and adjustments in market demands. Critically driving this shift is the emergence of artificial intelligence and the expansion of the gig economy. There is an intriguing symbiosis in the combination of these two movements, where AI serves as a tool to enable, facilitate, and enhance how freelancers work.

5.1. AI, A Matchmaker for the Job Market

Perhaps the most evident way AI technology has improved the lives of freelancers is by matching them with relevant work opportunities. AI-powered platforms use sophisticated machine learning algorithms to parse through job postings, analyze and understand job seekers' skills, interests, and availability, then match them with the ideal gigs.

This matchmaking process goes beyond merely scanning keywords in a job description or a worker's profile. AI considers variables such as industry trends, job popularity, pay scales, and requirements for skills and experiences. The result is a highly personalized job-seeking experience, where each worker receives a curated list of positions best suited to them.

Such effective matchmaking is mutually beneficial. For companies, it ensures they find the most suitable candidates faster and reduce recruitment costs, while for freelancers, it increases their visibility and chances of securing quality gigs.

File sharing platforms like Dropbox and Google Drive use AI to organize, search, and expand freelancers' work utilities. For joint projects involving multiple team members, these capabilities can boost collaboration and streamline workflows.

5.2. Automating Tedious Tasks

AI tools have also become valuable allies in eliminating or greatly reducing manual, laborious tasks, thereby increasing productivity. Such mundane duties include scheduling meetings, creating invoices, managing emails, or tracking work hours.

Virtual assistants like Alexa, Siri, or Google Assistant use AI to manage a freelancer's personal and work life alike, so they can focus more on performing strenuous professional tasks. On the other hand, specialized AI tools such as AND CO, FreshBooks, or QuickBooks automate invoicing and account management, mitigating the stress associated with these operations.

This automation is not limited to organizational aspects; it also splashes into the creative process. For instance, platforms like Canva use AI to simplify and automate graphic design, allowing freelancers who are not design professionals to create quality visuals with ease.

5.3. Enhancing Skill Development

The Internet is a vast playground offering a treasure trove of resources for those willing to explore and learn. AI platforms are increasingly becoming prominent in enabling freelancers to improve or learn new skills, thanks to intelligent tutoring systems or AI-powered educational platforms.

Artificial intelligence can compile, curate, and present personalized learning pathways based on a freelancer's aspirations, current abilities, or areas of improvement. It can assess a learner's strengths and weaknesses, adapting the curriculum to them.

Coursera and Udemy, for instance, utilize AI to provide personalized learning experiences, recommendations for courses, and assessments based on the learner's progress. This personalization fosters more meaningful learning, thus benefiting freelancers in rapidly acquiring or enhancing skills required for their job market.

5.4. Safeguarding Freelancer Rights

The gig economy comes with an ache for many freelancers - a lack of systemic protections - leading to challenges such as uncompensated work hours, payment delays, or unfulfilled contracts. However, AI is making its way to equip freelancers with tools to safeguard their rights.

AI-based apps are emerging to track work hours accurately, automatically generate invoices based on these hours, and send reminders to clients. Platforms also employ AI to ensure adherence to contracts by automatically detecting deviations and alerting the freelancer immediately.

5.5. The Challenges Ahead

Despite the advancements, AI and the gig economy have their share of challenges. The increasing automation of tasks begs the question, which jobs will remain for human freelancers? How can the gig economy maintain a balance between human intelligence and artificial intelligence?

Additionally, privacy concerns arise, as AI systems collect, analyze, and store vast amounts of personal data from freelancers. An increased need for regulations and legislation is evident to address these concerns.

5.6. Concluding Thoughts

AI technology is undeniably aiding in improving the gig environment for freelancers. With machine learning, predictive analytics, and sophisticated algorithms, AI platforms can enhance freelancers' experience, right from sourcing work opportunities to task automation, skill enhancement, and rights protection. However, as we continue to dabble in this brave new world, it's essential to also look at the challenges and work towards striking a balance between the powers of AI and the intrinsic strengths of the human workforce.

Chapter 6. Freelancers' Opportunities in the AI-driven Gig Economy

The transformation of the global economy characterized by the rise of freelance work and the influence of Artificial Intelligence (AI) has created myriad opportunities for agile and tech-savvy professionals. This chapter seeks to explore in-depth these opportunities, as well as offer practical insights on how freelancers can best take advantage of them.

6.1. Riding the AI-driven Gig Economy Wave

The AI-driven gig economy represents a shift from traditional, location-based work to a more fluid and flexible model. This paradigm change is an outcome of advancements in AI technology, combined with the changing demographics and expectations of the modern labor force. The gig economy, primarily characterized by short-term contracts or freelance work, ordinarily provides many benefits: flexible schedules, independence, diversified portfolios — but in combination with AI, it presents a whole new dimension of opportunities.

AI can empower the gig economy in a three-fold manner: improved efficiency, greater personalization, and the creation of new jobs and roles. It can automate repetitive tasks, freeing up time for freelancers to focus on providing more value and nuanced offerings to their clients. Furthermore, AI can empower personalization of freelance services, tailored to client needs and increased accessibility to international markets.

6.2. Capitalizing on Virtual Talents and Remote Working

AI-powered platforms are making it easier for freelancers to find gigs that align with their skills, interests, and desired rates. Digital platforms such as Fiverr, Upwork, and Freelancer use AI and machine learning (ML) technologies to match freelancers with prospective clients. AI can analyze vast amounts of data to determine the best fit between freelancers and gigs, thus reducing the search time and increasing probabilities of satisfaction on both sides.

Simultaneously, AI has democratized access to international talent and global gigs. Through improved communication, collaboration, and project management tools embedded with AI features, freelancers can work from any corner of the world, breaking the barriers of geographical constraints. They can interface with clients in different time-zones, using AI-powered chatbots for servicing queries, online collaboration tools for work synchronization, and teleconferencing for direct interactions.

6.3. Embracing AI Enhancement Opportunities

AI augmentation—where AI enhances human intelligence instead of replacing it—is another significant area of opportunity for freelancers. This prospect is particularly noteworthy in creative fields such as writing, design, and multimedia editing, where AI tools can assist in brainstorming, organizing ideas, and optimizing the efficiency of creative processes. AI-powered tools such as automatic video editing software, text generation and editing AI (like Grammarly or Hemingway Editor), and AI design assistance tools provide a powerful boost to freelancers' productivity. They enhance the overall quality of deliverables while significantly reducing the time spent on routine tasks.

6.4. Adapting to New AI-Influenced Roles

Amidst fears of AI replacing humans, it is crucial to remember that AI also engenders fresh roles. AI's increasing influence translates into a massive need for AI specialists and trainers who can build, manage, and debug these complex systems. These roles are typically high-paying, and freelancers with relevant skills can immensely benefit from this demand. Furthermore, there is an increased need for 'AI translators', professionals who can communicate complex AI concepts in a simplified, accessible language, bridging the gap between technologists and the general business or customer population.

Additionally, as businesses integrate more AI technologies, there is an increased demand for data science, data analysis, and machine learning specialists who can gather, process, analyze, and interpret increasingly large amounts of data. As freelance workers, data professionals can offer their services to multiple clients simultaneously, optimizing their earnings and exposure to a variety of projects.

6.5. Mitigating Challenges in the AI-Driven Gig Economy

While there are many opportunities, freelancers need to understand and navigate the unique challenges posed by the AI-driven gig economy. Both it and AI are disruptive forces, changing how work is done, reinforcing the necessity for freelancers to be agile and continually updated in their skills and understanding of industry trends. Staying ahead of the AI curve requires proactive measures, including attending webinars and courses, following top AI influencers and resources, and learning how to manipulate AI tools to their advantage. Understanding AI ethics and advocacy is also crucial, as these areas will shape the future of AI technologies.

In conclusion, the AI-driven gig economy represents a vast reservoir of opportunities for freelancers, who are willing to adapt and evolve with this transformative wave. By staying flexible, reskilling continuously, and leveraging AI's power to augment their work, freelancers can capitalize on the opportunities presented, ensuring success in this brave new world.

Chapter 7. Riding the AI Wave: Enhancing Freelance Opportunities

Artificial Intelligence (AI) is propelling us into a future where the way we work and the work that we do is being totally redefined. Gone are the days when workers could only choose between full-time employment and traditional self-employment. The rise of the "gig economy" has provided a new model where workers can choose freelance work on a project-by-project basis, facilitated by platforms that bring together supply and demand. AI has the potential to supercharge this shift, bringing new opportunities and also new challenges for freelancers.

7.1. The Growing Gig Economy

The gig economy is an environment in which temporary positions are commonplace and companies contract with independent workers for short-term engagements. It has been growing rapidly, driven by global businesses adopting flexible working models that optimize cost efficiencies and productivity. It is estimated that in the US alone, 35% of workers are now freelancers.

This new model of work offers a number of benefits for workers, including flexibility, freedom to choose the most interesting projects and the potential for higher earnings. However, it also brings challenges, not least in terms of job security, mastery of new technologies, and a need for continuous learning and skilling.

7.2. AI: Reinventing Work

AI is an umbrella term that refers to machines, or computing systems, that exhibit intelligent behavior capable of handling complex tasks. This could range from understanding human speech to playing chess, identifying disease symptoms to driving cars. When applied to work, AI can drive efficiencies and productivity, while also reinventing roles and creating new opportunities.

This automation of routine tasks by AI liberates human time for more complex and creative tasks. For freelancers, this can mean not only that AI automates routine tasks, but also that it creates new opportunities as clients seek to implement these technologies.

7.3. AI Platforms: The New Marketplace

Emerging AI-powered platforms are rapidly becoming the marketplace of choice for freelancers. These platforms, harnessing the power of AI and machine learning, are far more efficient in matching supply with demand than traditional job boards.

AI algorithms can make more nuanced matches between freelancers and projects, taking into account a wide range of factors beyond just skill sets — right down to work style preferences or passion for a particular sector. For freelancers, these platforms offer a more targeted, efficient, and potentially rewarding way to find work.

7.4. Navigating Challenges

While AI brings many opportunities, it also presents challenges for freelancers. One significant challenge is the constantly evolving nature of AI technologies, which requires a commitment to lifelong learning. Freelancers must remain up to date with the latest AI tools and trends, as well as the skill sets required to use them.

Moreover, as AI automates some tasks, there will be a shift in the types of skills that are in demand. Freelancers must anticipate and adapt to these changes. This may involve reskilling or upskilling to develop new areas of expertise.

Freelancers also need to understand the ethical and societal implications of AI. As AI systems become more sophisticated, they are increasingly making decisions that used to be the exclusive domain of humans. This raises questions about accountability, bias, privacy and other issues.

7.5. Thriving in the AI-Age

Despite the challenges, freelancers can take proactive steps to thrive in the AI-driven gig economy. First, they should focus on learning new AI skills and continuously updating their knowledge. This could mean attending webinars, taking MOOC courses, or even seeking advanced degrees.

Differentiation is also key. As AI becomes commonplace, freelancers need to distinguish themselves from the crowd. This could mean developing a niche specialization, or incorporating AI into their offering in a unique way.

Lastly, freelancers should consider how AI can augment their own work. This could be through using AI-powered tools to enhance productivity, or by exploring how AI solutions can offer added value for clients.

With AI bringing a wave of changes to the gig economy, those who adapt and harness its potential will find themselves with a competitive edge. By investing in learning, adapting with the market, and leveraging AI, freelancers can ride the tide of change and continue to thrive.

Chapter 8. Challenges for Freelancers in the Gig Economy

Guiding the journey of the modern freelance worker are a set of distinct challenges that demand particular attention. These tend to cut across realms as diverse but intertwined as: navigating digital platforms, establishing a reliable work-life balance, securing fair remuneration, and engaging with AI-driven technologies.

8.1. Understanding Digital Platforms

At the heart of the gig economy are the multitude of digital platforms that facilitate the matchmaking between freelancers and clients. Websites such as Upwork, Fiverr, and Freelancer have established comprehensive systems dedicated to the provision of a multitude of services, ranging from graphic design to coding.

However, these platforms come with a learning curve. The challenge begins with understanding the workings of these various platforms, each with their own sets of rules, encapsulated in the fine print of their extensive terms and conditions. Misunderstanding or overlooking these rules can lead to mishaps, disputes, or even suspensions. Furthermore, each platform has its own culture, influencing the sort of projects posted, the way in which freelancers pitch for work, and how communication with clients is managed.

An additional complication arises in the form of algorithms that manage these platforms. Notably, these algorithms tend to favor individuals already successful within the platform, creating a difficulty for newcomers who are yet to build their profiles and reviews.

8.2. Balancing Work and Life

For many, the premise of freelancing is built upon the allure of flexibility. Yet, despite the inherent freedom, freelancers commonly struggle to maintain a solid work-life balance. This challenge arises for a few reasons.

Firstly, irregular working hours can bleed into personal time. With clients potentially coming from different time zones, it is common for freelancers to adjust their schedule to accommodate their client's convenience. Secondly, securing enough work can lead freelancers to overcommit, taking on too many projects and working long hours to meet deadlines, hence sacrificing downtime and personal life.

Moreover, the line between 'work' and 'life' can become blurred, especially for those working from home. Without the boundaries provided by a conventional office environment, home can become linked with work-related stress, encumbering relaxation and ultimately, productivity.

8.3. Financial Uncertainty and Fair Remuneration

Financial uncertainty is another major challenge in freelance work. Unlike salaried employees, gig workers must constantly search for new gigs as their existing projects complete. A term unique to the gig economy, 'feast or famine,' illustrates this cycle of having plenty of work followed by periods of scant or nil opportunities. This lack of consistent income presents the freelancer with a good deal of financial stress, impacting their ability to manage regular bills or secure loans.

Pricing one's services adequately is another financial challenge freelancers need to grapple with. Undervaluing work is common among new freelancers eager to garner positive reviews and repeat clients. However, this can inadvertently set a low standard that becomes difficult to raise. On the other hand, overpricing may deter potential work. Finding the sweet spot that not only remunerates fairly but is also attractive to clients is tricky but crucial.

As platforms take their cut from the freelancer's earnings, understanding these deductions and saving for expenses like taxes and insurance adds to the financial precariousness.

8.4. Engaging with AI-Driven Technologies

Lastly, a central theme in freelancing is the advent of AI within the work ecosystem. Artificial Intelligence is augmenting the range of services provided in the gig economy. More and more companies are adopting AI-based systems for tasks like customer service, design, or content creation, which previously required human involvement.

This reliance on AI often displaces human labor in certain tasks. Therefore, there is a need for freelancers to stay updated with the technological trends and upgrade their skills to remain relevant and competitive. The challenge here is twofold: finding reliable resources to learn from, and finding the time to do so whilst managing ongoing projects.

In conclusion, navigating the gig economy as a freelancer is filled with distinct challenges. Freelancers must learn to traverse digital platforms effectively, balance their work-life dynamics, manage financial uncertainty, and engage proactively with growing AI presence in their fields. Overcoming these challenges is no small feat, but is crucial in harnessing the opportunities in the evolving work sector.

Chapter 9. The Downside of AI: Implications for Freelancers

As technological advancements continue to shape the ways we work, the influence of Artificial Intelligence (AI) in the gig economy has been met with widespread acclaim for its ability to generate incredible opportunity. However, it's equally important to consider the challenges and complexities that these changes introduce, particularly for freelancers navigating this new landscape.

9.1. Impersonal Nature of AI

A significant concern regarding AI's role in the gig economy centers on its impersonal nature. While technology can facilitate connections between freelancers and clients, it lacks the human touch. Emotional intelligence, which encompasses empathy, understanding, and interpersonal connection, remains fundamentally human, and while progress has been made in AI's ability to mimic these aspects, it remains far from matching the intricacies of human emotion. This can lead to communication challenges between clients and freelancers, misunderstandings, and ultimately, dissatisfaction on either side.

Frequent interactions with AI can also lead to reduced human interaction, causing feelings of isolation for independent workers. This absence of personal exchange can compromise mental wellbeing over time, highlighting the importance of maintaining human connections in freelance work environments.

9.2. Algorithm Decisions and Unfair Competition

One keenly felt disadvantage sees AI-powered algorithms increasingly making critical decisions about who gets certain gig jobs. These algorithms often consider factors such as response rates and completion times to rate freelancers, pushing for a focus on quantity over quality. Consequently, those unable to maintain pace may find their job prospects dwindling. This environment promotes intense competition, fostering a culture of constant availability and rapid turnaround - a lifestyle that not all freelancers desire or can maintain.

AI technology could potentially lead to unfair competition, such as 'AI-powered gig workers.' For instance, chatbots and writing algorithms, like AI content generators, can produce vast amounts of written content in a short timeframe, presenting a daunting competitive front for human freelancers.

9.3. Job Insecurity and Diminished Bargaining Power

The precarious nature of gig work becomes more intensified in the wake of AI. It creates a systemic shift where jobs are perceived not as long-term contracts but as short-term tasks, leading to instability for freelancers. Coupled with that is an inherent risk of AI advancements making certain freelance skills redundant, creating a cloud of job insecurity for many independent workers.

The gig economy is infamous for unequal relationships between workers and platforms. AI applications compound this by further diminishing individual bargaining power. When decisions are made by unaccountable algorithms, it can be challenging for freelancers to negotiate fair pay and working conditions. Moreover, since most platforms set the price for gigs, freelancers have limited options to compete on anything but cost, leading to potential underpricing of their skills.

9.4. Privacy Concerns and Data Security

In a world where data is currency, the role of AI in managing and controlling vast amounts of personal and professional information holds implications for freelancers. Data breaches, misuse, or unethical use of data by gig platforms could lead to severe privacy concerns. Considering the data-centric nature of AI, freelancers must be more vigilant about data security, often requiring knowledge and skills beyond their primary competencies.

9.5. Skill Evolution Mandate

The advent of AI demands that freelancers continuously evolve their skills to stay relevant. As AI algorithms become more intelligent and autonomous, freelancers are compelled to upskill and reskill, ensuring that their competencies aren't replaced by machines. This mandate introduces significant pressure and can be an uphill struggle given the pace at which AI is advancing.

While AI stands to revolutionize the gig economy, its implications possess an undeniable gravity. As we continue to peel back the layers of the digital-led gig economy, it is crucial to balance tech advancements with ethical considerations, mitigating the potential downside while maximizing the opportunities. Freelancers must stay educated on these implications to successfully navigate the waters in this brave new world.

Chapter 10. Overcoming Challenges: Strategies for Success in the AI-enabled Gig Economy

The AI-enabled gig economy promises a wealth of opportunities for freelancers, but it also serves up unique obstacles that need to be managed. Building a successful freelance career in this environment requires the development of a variety of strategies, designed both to leverage the potential benefits and to counterbalance the potential drawbacks of this new workspace. In the following pages, we will delve into these strategies, exploring how freelancers can maximize opportunities and overcome challenges in the AI-enabled gig economy.

10.1. Understanding AI and Its Potential in Your Field

One of the first steps towards success in the AI-enabled gig economy is to develop a solid understanding of Artificial Intelligence and its relevance to your field of work. AI is far from a uniform tool; its capabilities can vary greatly, and its applications are virtually endless. Being aware of how AI techniques, such as machine learning, natural language processing, robotic process automation, and predictive analytics, can enhance your services is essential. This understanding will not only allow you to carve a niche for yourself in the gig economy but also enable you to provide value-added services to your clients.

Consider taking online courses, attending seminars, and reading case studies to familiarize yourself with AI. Identify its usage in your field or look at how others have integrated AI successfully in their offerings. By doing so, you'll be stepping forward into a world brimming with opportunities previously unimagined.

10.2. Adapting to Technology: Tools & Platforms

The proliferation of online platforms and digital tools tailored for freelancers is a hallmark of the gig economy. Being adept at navigating these tools can be a significant advantage. Checking and bidding for tasks, communicating with clients, or managing your workflow, all happens digitally. Familiarity with project management tools like Trello, Slack, or Asana, proficiency in using communication platforms like Zoom or Microsoft Teams, and understanding gig-specific platforms like Fiverr, Upwork, or Freelancer can make the difference between struggling and thriving.

In an AI-enabled gig economy, employing AI-powered tools can also significantly ramp up your productivity. Whether it be Grammarly for writers, Adobe Sensei for creatives, or Kuki AI for customer service representatives, using such tools can drastically improve the quality of your work and increase your efficiency.

10.3. Creating a Personal Brand

In a sea of freelancers, standing out is a daunting task but also a necessity. Building a personal brand sets you apart, providing an identity that can be synonymous with quality, reliability, professionalism, or any attribute you wish to emphasize.

Use social media platforms like LinkedIn, Instagram, or Twitter to showcase your portfolio, share testimonials, and regularly engage with your audience. Don't overlook the potential of AI-driven analytics these platforms provide. They can furnish you with detailed insights on audience engagement, helping you to tailor your marketing messages and fostering a deft combination of human creativity and AI-generated data to drive your personal branding.

10.4. Financial Management

A significant challenge freelancers face is financial instability. Irregular income, lack of job security, and the absence of conventional benefits often make financial management problematic. It's essential for freelance workers to develop financial discipline and planning.

Create a budget considering all your expenses, fluctuating income, and potential dry spells. Utilize personal finance apps or AI-enhanced tools like Mint, Quicken, or TurboTax to keep track of earnings, savings, taxes, and expenses. Ensure setting aside a portion of your income for emergency savings, insurance, and retirement.

10.5. Navigating Legal and Tax Obligations

The gig economy straddles various legal and tax jurisdictions, making it essential for freelancers to understand this complex landscape. Depending on where your clients are located, or the platforms you use, you may be subject to different rules and regulations.

Utilize AI-driven tools like LegalZoom or TurboTax that can help navigate through these complex waters, providing platform-specific or location-specific legal and tax advice.

10.6. Skill Enhancement and Lifelong Learning

In the current, fast-moving digital landscape, skills needed today might be obsolete tomorrow. Freelancers must adopt a mindset of lifelong learning. Online courses, webinars, podcasts, and workshops are excellent resources for maintaining relevancy in the face of evolving technology.

Furthermore, many traditional roles have seen a fusion with AI, creating new roles like AI-Based Digital Marketers or AI Business Analysts. Proactively learning AI and combining it with your traditional skills can open up a niche rarely filled by others.

In conclusion, the AI-enabled gig economy offers a brave new world of work, a world filled with numerous opportunities and unique challenges. By adopting these strategies, independent workers can harness the potential AI promises and build a fulfilling, successful career in the gig economy. As we step further into the digital future, change is inevitable, and the ability to adapt and evolve will be the real measure of success.

Chapter 11. Looking Forward: The Future of AI and the Gig Economy for Freelancers

The freelance economy has been escalating in recent years, and with the advent of Artificial Intelligence (AI), a new set of opportunities and challenges have arisen. As we peek into the crystal ball, some predictions start to emerge, shaping the future of AI and the gig economy for freelancers.

11.1. The Maturation of AI and Its Impact

AI has been gradually transforming countless sectors, and the freelance industry is no exception. Thanks to AI, freelancers can now benefit from advanced technology such as intelligent automation of routine tasks, enhancing productivity. For instance, AI-powered tools for content creation, graphic design, and programming can significantly reduce the time freelancers spent to accomplish their tasks, thus increasing their efficiency.

Moreover, AI can be used for increasing connectivity and job discovery. An AI system can potentially analyze a freelancer's skills, interests, and history, and connect them with appropriate tasks available worldwide. This not only diversifies the work pool but also adds a personal touch to job hunting, making the process less strenuous and more rewarding.

However, as AI matures, it also brings forth challenges. With AI showing potential in playing an active role in creative fields, there is a fear that certain jobs might be under threat. Freelancers need to continuously upgrade their skills to stay relevant in this dynamic environment.

11.2. Tapping Into AI Services

AI services are also poised to become significant partners for freelancers. Companies such as Fiverr and Upwork are implementing AI systems to suggest jobs to freelancers that they might be interested in, based on their previous jobs and skillsets. This automation and personalization of task allocation are set to improve the freelancers' experience ethically.

On the flip side, the rising use of AI services exposes a notable vulnerability—privacy concerns. Given the reliance on data, increasing vigilance will be required to ensure data security and privacy, thus demanding a more robust data protection system.

11.3. Shaping Up the Skills

Labelling AI as an adversary won't serve freelance professionals well. Rather, viewing it as a new skillset to incorporate into their repertoire will transform them into more robust, future-ready professionals. Learning to work along with AI, leveraging its strengths while compensating for its weaknesses, is probably a more productive and lucrative approach to incorporate AI into freelance work.

Understanding AI, data science, and their practical use will be indispensable for future freelancers, regardless of the field they are in. For instance, graphic designers might need to understand how to use AI design tools while writers might need to be aware of the latest AI writing aids and adjust their style accordingly.

11.4. The Dawn of the AI-Empowered Freelancer

In a nutshell, the future of freelancing in the AI-dominated era is promising yet challenging. Embracing rather than fearing AI, upgrading skills, maintaining data privacy and getting the best out of AI-powered platforms will be elementary in this journey.

At the dawn of this new era, freelancers equipped with an understanding of AI will be a step ahead in this competitive environment. The collaboration of humans and AI promises to bring the best of both worlds. AI provides scalability, speed and precision, humans bring creativity, contextual understanding, and strategic intuition.

With such collaborations, the boundaries of what a freelancer can achieve will be expanded. AI will not be an active player replacing human workforces but a tool, which, if used correctly, can expand the boundaries of accomplishment.

11.5. Preparing for the Future

In the light of the above, it's indispensable for freelancers and gig workers to be prepared for these transformations. Learning to use AI tools and understanding data security should be prioritized in their to-do list.

Freelancers need to stay updated with AI developments in their field and attend relevant workshops, webinars and online courses in the context of AI. Moreover, joining a community of freelancers where insights, challenges, and discussions about AI's unfolding role in freelance work are common, would be instrumental.

To wrap up, the future of AI and the gig economy seems promising yet challenging for freelancers; they must keep hustling, keep learning, and keep adapting. The widespread adoption of AI in the gig economy is an evolutionary process, and freelancers, as proactive players, need to adapt to keep pace with this revolution. It's time to step out of comfort zones, embrace and master new technologies, and build a sustainable career in this rapidly evolving digital world. The future waits to be written with code and creativity.